# EARN PASSIVELY LEARNING E-BOOK PUBLISHING

Mrs Esther Ohakim

Copyright © 2o21 Mrs Esther ohakim

All rights reserved

The characters and events portrayed in this book are fictitious. Any similarity to real persons, living or dead, is coincidental and not intended by the author.

No part of this book may be reproduced, or stored in a retrieval system, or transmitted in any form or by any means, electronic, mechanical, photocopying, recording, or otherwise, without express written permission of the publisher.

ISBN:9798750042111

Cover design by: Art Painter
Library of Congress Control Number: 2018675309
Printed in the United States of America

*I humbly dedicate this book to the Holy Trinity: God the father, the son my advocate and the Holy spirit, who has been and is still my teacher, inspiration and wisdom.*

# CONTENTS

Title Page

Copyright

Dedication

Introduction

| | |
|---|---:|
| CHAPTER ONE | 1 |
| CHAPTER TWO | 2 |
| CHAPTER THREE | 4 |
| CHAPTER FOUR | 6 |
| CHAPTER FIVE | 11 |
| CHAPTER SIX | 13 |
| CHAPTER SEVEN | 15 |
| CHAPTER EIGHT | 19 |
| CHAPTER NINE | 22 |
| CHAPTER TEN | 25 |
| CHAPTER ELEVEN | 26 |
| CHAPTER TWELVE | 28 |
| CHAPTER THIRTEEN | 29 |
| CHAPTER FOURTEEN | 31 |
| CHAPTER FIFTEEN | 36 |
| CHAPTER SIXTEEN | 37 |

| | |
|---|---|
| CHAPTER SEVENTEEN | 38 |
| CHAPTER EIGHTEEN | 39 |
| CHAPTER NINETEEN | 40 |
| Acknowledgement | 41 |
| About The Author | 43 |
| Books By This Author | 45 |

# INTRODUCTION

The very fact that you got interested and picked up this book to go through it is an indication you are aware that digital gold mine exists and only those who know the "how" about it get to become beneficiaries.

Hence, the interest to go through this beautiful piece
Today, you are beginning a Journey- a digital journey.
A journey that will bring about liberation. One that will empower you, broaden your horizon and position you for success.

As you continue reading, you will learn the basic method in the art of E-book Creation and Publishing on Amazon.
You will also learn how to publish on Amazon and earn. So, this book will help you learn in other to earn passively.
The digital world is a fast world and speed is everything. Therefore, you must learn fast and join the train.

# CHAPTER ONE

*CREATING A STRONG BOOK*

Talking about a strong and purposeful writing. A strong write up is one that when published, it is easily acceptable by all and sought after by many because of its rich content. Such works as "Things fall Apart by Chinua Achebe, The Confessions by St. Augustine," etc are examples of a strong book having a definite purpose.

A strong book can easily become a BEST SELLER, that is a book that sells like wild fire, sought by many, for example; if a book sells 10,000 copies over a short period, it is a best seller. A good example is the book written by Barack Obama, "The Promised Land" it became a BEST SELLER, as it sold thousands within a short period.

Your work too can be a best seller, if and only if you give it your best and the earning is unending at just a single effort. This is one of the ways you make a passive income for life.

Do you know children books are BEST SELLERS too? So no matter what you are writing on, always give it your best, you can write it in a simple manner, but let the message be clear.

# CHAPTER TWO

*STEPS IN WRITING A BOOK*

1. Get really clear on the topic you want to write on, your book must have a purpose
2. Create the outline for your book
3. Block out your calendar to write your book. Do not allow the enemy to stop you by your consistent procrastination. Avoid distractions which hinder you from taking actions; examples are calls, hangouts with friends, visitations, etc. if you have to put your phone on airplane mode so people can't contact you for that specific number of hours you have designated to work on your book, go ahead!
4. Sit down and write your book

The world has gone digital and It is the reason you are reading this book
you do not want to be left behind. Amazon has made it easier for everyone to publish their books online

Do you know that Amazon started from a garage?

Yes, from a garage in 1994, 27 years ago.

Today Jeff Bezos, the founder is the second richest man in the world according to Forbes Magazine, he didn't give up.
In 2001 he had a serious challenge that made him lay off over 1000 workers, but he was not discouraged.
He pushed on and today we all want to get on that platform

and also earn like him.

Recently, On July 5th 2021, he stepped down as CEO, a position he held for 27 years, he handed over to Andrew Jassy and he is now in the Executive chair, you too can be like and even more than the owner of Amazon. You are almost there, but not yet.

# CHAPTER THREE

*E-BOOK*

You already know what an e-book is. Simply put, it is an Electronic version of a book, Call it the soft copy of a book. Many books today are in the electronic version, as an author if you don't have your book in an electronic version you are actually lagging behind for with e-books you reach a larger audience.

Your book is not only sold in your current city/location; it will be available globally.

This is the platform amazon gives to you. That is why so many persons are looking for online publishers to get their books online.

This is the fastest way your book can be a bestseller.

In this digital journey, I want to charge our mind towards achieving goals especially the goal of publishing on a global platform;

"LEAVING YOUR COMFORT ZONE"

I left my comfort zone to learn this art. This is a beautiful skill, if you are focused, you will enjoy it for life, and will always thank God for it.

You should know that there is ability in everyone and everything to succeed if only it is identified. I am saying this is to spur you not to quit especially when the practical aspect starts properly, so it is like a red flag beforehand and that is the very point where many want to give up.

Therefore, I encourage you today never to give up in anything worthwhile not even in this digital journey. For the fact I learnt it and am doing it, you too can do it.

When you learn how to create and publish an e-book, you can easily write and publish in your name or you get clients who will ask you to and you collect good royalties from them.

Jeff Bezos the owner of Amazon on whose platform you will be creating and publishing your e-book to avail it globally for readers and researchers is one of the richest men on earth. In fact, he is the second richest man in the world today according to Forbes, he is worth $200 billion as of today, convert his worth to your local currency and check out his worth. Also, many around the globe are benefiting from him through his platform; Amazon.

How did he get here? It all started with a dream and the determination to push through against all odds and challenges, for we can all do anything we set our minds to do or achieve. It is about finding solutions rather than giving complains, quitting or loosing hope which means you have been defeated. That's why I told you earlier that you must be intentional in this digital journey.

You are about to get into the next stage of e-book creation and publishing (basic method and advance method) in order to earn but it comes with its own crucible challenge.

The crucible, this can be a title of a strong book you know. The crucible is the final test before you become a marine. It is meant to test the physical, mental and moral preparedness of every recruit

The next stages will test your capability and readiness for success. If you do not complete the crucible test you cannot take the oath of the marines and you cannot be enlisted as A US marine. If you do not overcome the crucible challenge in the learning of creation and publishing of e-book, you will definitely miss the opportunity of having a means or another means of passive earning.

# CHAPTER FOUR

*INTRODUCTION TO AMAZON TEMPLATES (BASIC METHOD)*

Now publishing on Amazon requires some basic ground rules, if not your book will be rejected.

A template is a guide that a writer follows while writing an article, a book, a letter, etc.

I like been pragmatic, so would like you to be practical with this. Why not get your writing material and try pen down some key notes, you shall use it for practice in the amazon kdp after opening an account in the platform.

Yes! You are going to open an amazon kdp account if you don't have one, that is the platform for creation and publishing of your e-books if you want it to sell globally. Please start preparing your notes, you will be using it to learn how to publish on amazon.

A template helps the writer follow a specific structure and write faster. Templates are important because they can save you lots of time and keep your work organized especially if you're a beginner. It gives you a clear pattern, a clear route to follow while writing, blogging, etc.

We have templates for writing letters

We have templates for writing marketing emails, etc

  We have The Template that Amazon uses too

Amazon kdp has both paperback and hard cover manuscript templates for you already in Microsoft word to help you format your manuscript, it's the createspace formatting template.

Take a look at the screenshots below, they are template examples ������

# CHAPTER FIVE

*INTRODUCTION TO FORMATTING (BASIC METHOD)*

Now to formatting,

Simply put, the format is the layout of your template

We are going technical; remember you should not give up.

The format is the way your document looks and is visually organized. it addresses things like font selection, font size and presentation (like bold or italics), spacing, margins, alignment, columns, indentation, and lists.

You can see from the template given that it is already in the accepted format for publication on amazon, all you need do is highlighting, back spacing or deleting in order to paste in your copied content. While imputing your prepared notes do follow the pattern given below;

The following elements must be in your book for Amazon to accept it for publication

1. Cover page
2. Copyright page
3. Dedication, acknowledgement,
4. Table of contents
5. Introduction
6. Body (or Chapters).

7. Back page (about the author).

However, note that the order above isn't sacrosanct.

You may alter the order from items 3 to 5.

As you read on when you get to publishing, you will learn how to design your cover page from the many designs provided by amazon.

We are using a template so that amazon does not reject your manuscript, you just simply edit and input your write-ups. Just make sure you download it and input your notes in the template then save because that is the file you will upload and publish on Amazon, for practice.

# CHAPTER SIX

*MANUAL FORMATTING OF MANUSCRIPT (ADVANCE - METHOD)*

In this advance method we are to use a different formatting app/software known as **KINDLE CREATE SOFT WARE**.

To download it; go to kdp.amazon.com and choose the option download kindle create, choose either download to pc or download to mac. After which you give it some time to download the heavy file to your PC.

When you are done downloading your screen should look like the image below.

< Kindle Store

*Beautiful books, every time*

Professionally designed themes with chapter titles, drop caps and image placement options.

# CHAPTER SEVEN

*THE KINDLE AD-IN: SHOWS THE FEATURES OF THE KINDLE CREATE APP*

**The kindle** Add-in for Microsoft word is an easy way for authors to produce beautiful looking eBooks and paperbacks with professional styles for title pages, drop caps and chapter headings, all with the familiar Microsoft word interphase.

To get started, open your book in Microsoft word and select the kindle tab. Select Get started. This prepares your word document for best result as a kindle eBook and a 6 x 9 print paperback.

**Overview of the kindle Tab**

Before you get started, most of the styling features are grayed out, although you can preview your work by selecting the kindle previewer. After you get started, the following options are enabled on the kindle tab.

- **Insert into book:** Here you can insert one of several template pages, insert separators between transition in texts.
- **Apply common elements:** Here you can apply the styles and most frequently in a book
- Apply elements by type: Here you can apply all of the styles available in the Kindle Add-in, which are categorized into; Title page elements, book start and element

and book body elements.

- **Current Paragraph Formatting:** This section identifies the Kindle Add-in formatting that is been applied at the cursor location and allows you clear the formatting and return your selection to plain body text.

- **Review:** Here you can show or hide paragraph marks and other formatting symbols and preview your book in Kindle previewer

- **Prep for publish:** here you can add page headers and page numbers to the book

## ANATOMY OF A KINDLE BOOK

Kindle books are generally organized into the following divisions;

- Book title page: Displays book title, authors name and other publication information
- Front matter pages: these pages include introduction, Author's note, Acknowledgement, table of contents, etc.
- Part pages: A divider page to identify a new book part in a multi-part book
- Chapter pages: the text of the book
- Back matter pages: includes About the Author, Endnote, Appendix Bibliography

## FORMATTING YOUR BOOK IN KINDLE ADD-IN

In formatting your book in this modern software follow the guide below:

- Getting started
- Adding preformatted sample pages
- Selecting your theme
- Formatting your content

This has to do with;

>...formatting front matter and back matter pages
>...formatting your table of contents
>...formatting each chapter

- Preparing your book for publishing
- Previewing your book

Sample of your preview using this modern app would look like the screenshots below;

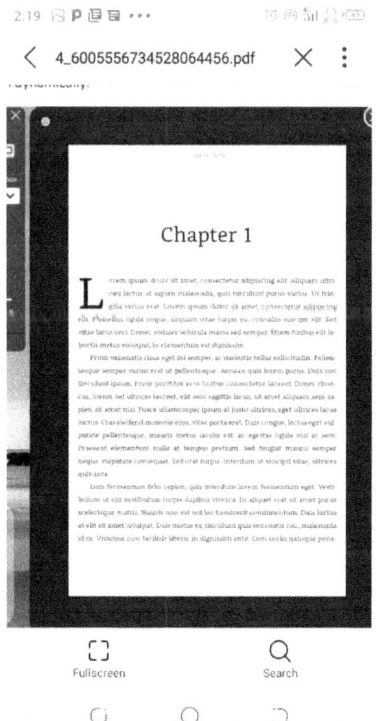

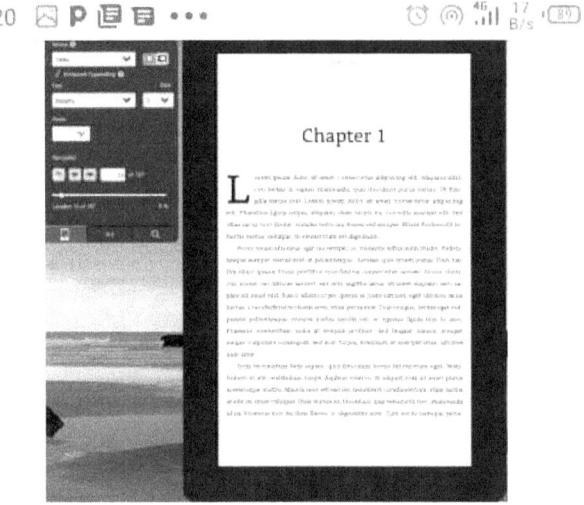

Figure 5: Kindle Previewer

There is also a Kindle interactive TOC view that allows you to navigate to the start of the chapter. To preview your book's Kindle Interactive TOC, select the list button at the bottom of the **Inspector** window as shown in Figure 6.

Kindle Add-In for Microsoft Word User Guide — version 0.97 Beta

Figure 6: Kindle Interactive TOC tab of Kindle Previewer

### 3.7 Getting Help

# CHAPTER EIGHT

*CREATING YOUR KDP ACCOUNT*

Kindle direct publishing (Kdp) is the publishing arm of Amazon that is concerned with publishing your book online and allows you to sell your e-book to amazon's massive audience, all for free. You create and upload while amazon sells it; in return you gain your royalties. After the sale you only give amazon 30% the remaining 70% is all yours.

If you already have an account with them, then no need to create another just log in. If you do not have one kindly go to Kdp.amazon.com to create yours.

You will be asked to fill a form with your details which includes name, country, address, phone number, etc.

Please ensure the phone number you are giving is the one in your phone because you will be sent a code for verification.

Take note of the portal code; The security measures in Amazon is tight, hence you would be sent an otp code to your phone, for you to type from your phone to the page.

Hence my advice initially to use your browser line, because amazon will seek your approval which you will do from your phone.

If you succeeded in opening an account in amazon kdp, what you have should look like the screenshot above.

Take note of the notification; your acct information is incomplete this will take us to our next stage.

## Two step verification of your account

This has to do with the getting paid aspect and filling your tax information.

If you have opened your account, try to fill the account information. In filling the information, On the Getting Paid session, you will notice that amazon does not recognize Nigerian banks in case you are in Nigeria and some other countries too. Therefore, for this basic stage just opt for cheque payments.

In filling the tax information, those with tax information especially those outside the U.S you can opt for I have a non-U. S and fill it if you have a tax ID in your country. For those without tax, you will have to uncheck the "I have a non-U. S" box and click on a suitable reason why you can't fill your tax details.

# CHAPTER NINE

*GUIDES TO E-BOOK COVER CREATION*

1. Log unto your account, locate the particular e-book you want to create cover for saved in the draft session of your kdp account.
2. Click on cover creator and fill in the three stages of form presented to you in order to process your e-book cover
3. Save and continue when done with each stage
4. When the "How to use cover creator" window pops up, click continue
5. This takes you to photo gallery; here you are to choose a particular image from the categories presented to you.
6. After choosing your image for the e-book cover save, the next stage is to choose the layout of your chosen image on the cover page, you are to explore this area as there are various colors to try, various fonts and patterns.
7. Then you save, continue, click on preview cover page, after which you finally save.
8. After taking a few seconds to process and link to your uploaded manuscript, it will be available on your kdp front page.

Note that you will receive a congratulatory notification in your email when your book comes live on amazon.

Note: To create an e-book cover you will need the following;
1. A concise about the author ready in MS Word
2. A concise about the book ready in MS Word

3. Image to create your cover. Its either you select from the kdp photo gallery or you use your own image from the computer.

Below are good samples of an e-book cover page;

# CHAPTER TEN

*GUIDES TO PAPERBACK COVER CREATION*

1. Go to the particular book whose paperback you want to create
2. Select cover creator like you did for the e-book cover
3. Then launch cover creator
4. Click continue on the "How to use cover creator" window
5. Choose an image from the photo gallery, under a particular category; weather food, science, technology, editorials, etc, which ever suites you.
6. The next is to choose your book design from options provided, edit the about the author, author's name, upload your picture, type in your about the book.
7. Author's image is to be uploaded from your computer where you have saved it
8. You then save all you have done, click preview, save and submit

Note: To create a paperback cover you will need the following;

1. A concise about the author ready in MS Word
2. A concise about the book ready in MS Word
3. Image to create your cover. Its either you select from the kdp photo gallery or you use your own image from the computer
4. The Author's image

# CHAPTER ELEVEN

*UPLOADING AND PUBLISHING YOUR E-BOOK*

I hope by now you are ready with your notes from previous readings in the format createspace formatting app for the basic method and kindle create app for the advance method. You are to download both of them. The kindle create app is for the publishing of professional books which meet global standard as it has so many modern features which makes your work unique. These features are not found in the createspace formatting app. Get ready for upload!

**How to Publish & Upload your e-Book**

Simple steps to follow:

1. Sign in into your kdp account through kdp.amazon.com

2. You will get to Your Account page. At the top you will find Bookshelf. Click on that.

3. Go to the icon kindle create

NB: Ensure your manuscript has been formatted in line with the Template you read about initially, CreateSpace Format Template.

4. When you click on that icon it will take you through three steps before you upload.

5.In the first step, you will fill details about your book and give a little description, like a summary people can see about your book when you are done you save and continue. You will also see the create your cover page 5icon for your eBook. You could pick an image from the gallery and design.

6. Upload your manuscript! Do practice it now...

# CHAPTER TWELVE

*DIFFERENCES BETWEEN E-BOOK AND PAPERBACK*

1. E-Books are electronic or digital books while paperbacks are hard copies or physical books
2. You publish your eBooks and paperbacks independently
3. It takes about 24 hours for your eBooks to come live on amazon
4. It takes about 72hours for your paperback to come live on amazon
5. The publishing of your eBooks and paperbacks are independent, even though they are the same manuscript but require different processors and have different processing.
6. You can link your eBooks to your paperbacks by clicking the 3dots or on either at your bookshelf and clicking link books by following the prompt

# CHAPTER THIRTEEN

*ISBN GENERATION*

It is advisable to get your ISBN from kdp before formatting your manuscript with the kindle create software. Also ensure your given ISBN is the one you pasted during formatting else you will encounter challenge while publishing.

You can either use your own ISBN procured from your country or request for free ISBN. The reason is because yours may not be recognized which will hinder the distribution of your books globally.

To get your free ISBN from kdp

1. Go to your book shelf
2. Start the paperback publishing process
3. When you click on start to publish paperback
4. Fill in the form provided until you get to the ISBN page
5. You will be asked if you want the kdp ISBN or not, then you click it and receive. You will need the ISBN at the kindle create app processing, while filling the copyright segment.

**ISBN MATCHING**

To do this effectively, copy the approval (ISBN) from your kdp account and paste during formatting with the kindle create app.

Note: you cannot use the kdp ISBN outside kdp. Go to your national library to get an ISBN if you wish to self-publish.

Please, do not add your ISBN to your unformatted manuscript. You are to use it to replace the default ISBN on the app. This is the reason you must get your ISBN before formatting.

# CHAPTER FOURTEEN

*PAYMENT METHODS / WITHDRAWALS*

1.PAYONEER

payoneer is the preferred bank of choice amongst many foreign authors who are not united states residents.

2.SIGN PROCESS

With payoneer sign up. Google payoneer, sign up with your email address,

create a password, verify your email address and fill out all the necessary

required details such as name, ID or passport number, residential address,

country of residence and banking details.

1.Type www.payoneer.com on your browser

2.Click register

3.Select the appropriate option from the drop-down box (individual)

4.Then select "get paid by international clients or market places".

5.Then click register

For the first interface fill in the following

1.Name

2.Surname

3. Email address

4. Re-enter Email address

5. Date of birth

6. Then click next

For second the next interface fill in the following details

1. Country of Residence

2. Address

3. Zip Code

4. Mobile Number

5. Verification Code sent to your mobile number

For the third interface, fill in the following details

1. Your email address

2. Your password

3. Re-enter password

4. Your security (2) questions

5. Your security (2) answers

6. Your ID or passport Number

7. Date of issue

8. Date of expiration

9. Random decode selection

For the fourth and final interface, fill in the following details

1. Your bank name

2. Your bank number 31

3. Indicate if it is cheque or savings

4. Swift code

6. And your registration is done.

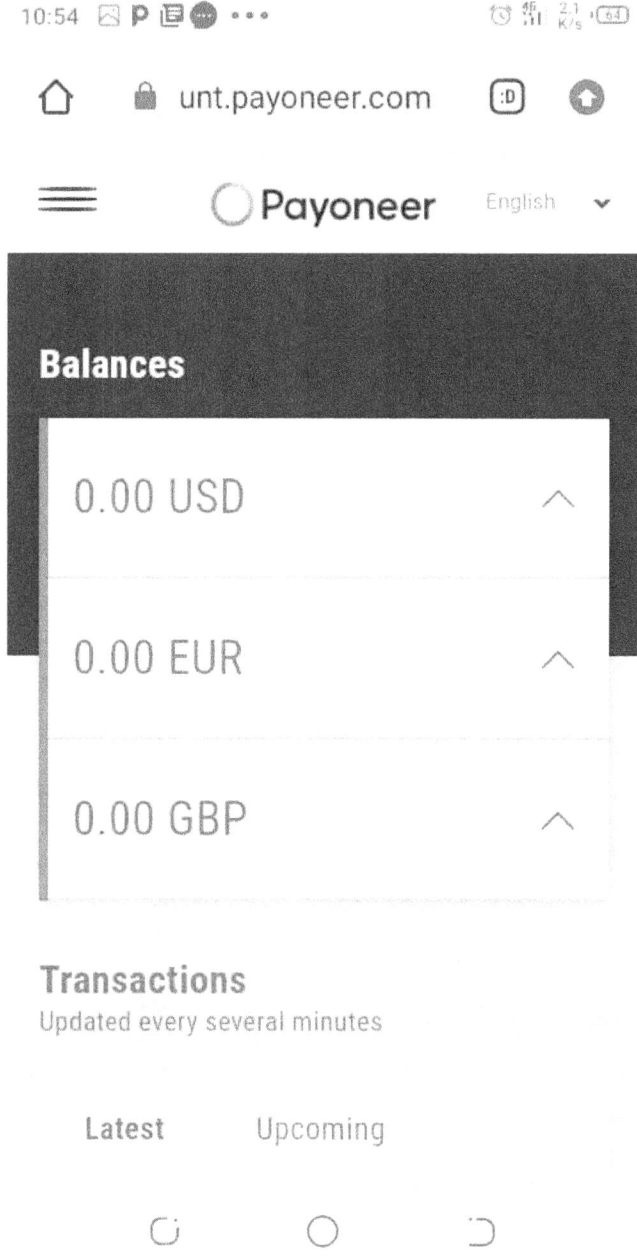

Once created, click on the USD option to capture the bank details that will be uploaded to kindle direct publishing. The details are the following

1. Bank Name

2. Band Address

3. Routing

4. Account Number Domiciled

5. Account Type

6. Reference Name

You will then launch your kindle direct publishing account and provide the

details such as name of the bank domiciled in the US with the address, account

type, account number and reference in the portion interface responsible for

payment. After updating your details, you will receive a successful prompt

which indicates that you have provided all the required information. You will now process to provide the details of your tax income number referred to TIN, this is if you haven't done it earlier when you opened the kdp account.

If your country's TIN is accepted by Kindle Direct Publishing, you can input it but when it does not accept your country of residence TIN, you must give an explanation of the reason why it is not acceptable. Once you have filled all the information required in the TIN section, your account will be given the go ahead to publish your books do the pricing and once the eBook has been purchased you will be notified of how much royalty you will be receiving for the purchase of your eBook.

Remember, payoneer acts as the intermediary bank between the

US and your local bank. And that is why is it extremely important to get this right

# CHAPTER FIFTEEN

*SALES, PROMOTIONS AND MARKETING*

This has to do with digital marketing, the cheapest of it is the one done by you through your social media platform; for example, your WhatsApp status, Facebook feed and story, your Instagram story and feed, twitter, etc.

As an author you should copy the link to your books and share to friends, families, groups and other social media feeds.

You can also engage kdp for their paid marketing services
You may as well engage digital marketers

You may also organize book launch, book reading, etc.

FURTHER CAUSES OF POOR SALES OF BOOKS

- Poor editing can kill a book
- Poor formatting can kill a book
- Poor design can kill a book
- Wrong publishing
- Poor contents
- Besides several others

Generally, you have to market and advertise your book. Selling is helping People buy.

# CHAPTER SIXTEEN

*MONETISATION EXERCISE*

Becoming an expert in this skill, you have a lot to gain. This is the sweetest
Part of having this skill. The earning part, which could become a means of passive income if you know what you are doing. You could become a Consultant and lend your knowledge in this field for a token.

You could also reproduce this knowledge in the lives of many by teaching them and leading them into training the younger generation all with a token.

It can become another stream of income or Side hustle for many.

# CHAPTER SEVENTEEN

*FAQ*

My paper back upload keeps returning as draft. It calls for trouble shooting

Answers
You should have previewed before publishing; this gives you the error message by the left pane of the of the previewer

You may not have edited the default content on your cover. Go back, hover the curser over the contents on the back and front and edit

ISBN- Mismatch; be sure ISBN used for the interior was allocated by kdp

Please be sure you actually used the kindle create software to edit your manuscript

In any case, after reviewing, just go back to your kdp account to publish

Above all, you may start the formatting and editing all over.

# CHAPTER EIGHTEEN

*Fixing of prices*

This should not be a source of undue confusion, anxiety and prolonged discussion.
Note the following;

1. You are the publisher
2. At the point of pricing kdp gives you the price limit
3. Besides 2 above, kdp has a button by the pricing board, where you click for analytics.
4. Above all be modest with pricing, as it's a free publishing package

On royalties plan you should have the 70%

On distribution

Kdp would manage that, but you can procure their promotional packages for wider range of sales, marketing and distribution.

# CHAPTER NINETEEN

*COPYRIGHT*

The issue of copyright is very important in publishing Amazon will not accept any material that has copyright issues.

plagiarism is a serious offense. If you are taking any material that is not yours ensure to reference it.

That is why you have been told how to get your free ISBN number and how to create your paperback book cover and interior.

# ACKNOWLEDGEMENT

My profound gratitude goes to God Almighty for I count it as both a privilege and an opportunity to author this insightful book.

I also appreciate my wonderful tutors who took me through the basic and master class of this course, Mrs Bridget Omoruyi and Mr Solomon Okpa aka Ogakpatakpata, you are a God sent indeed.

I truly and sincerely thank my husband for his understanding, motivation and huge support all through the period of my training and the putting together of this work, God bless you pleasure.

# ABOUT THE AUTHOR

## Mrs Esther Ohakim

Mrs Esther Ohakim is a humble keen lady who hails from Akokwa in Ideato Local Government Area of Imo state, Nigeria. She is a wife and a mother. A very thoughtful person who delights in expounding the deep things of life in order to give people an understanding and direction.

She is a well sort after e-publisher, a website developer, a content creator, a digital marketer and an author. She is also a motivational speaker and loves public health matters.

# BOOKS BY THIS AUTHOR

## Fundamentals On E-Book Publishing

This book is your number step by step guide to e-book creation and pubishing.you will learn how to open a kdp account, the amazon accepted template and how to use it, formatting, uploading your manuscript and choosing your cover page. its very easy to understand, descriptive pictures are inclusive.

## Understanding The Power Of Your Mind

Understanding the power of your mind tells you how your mind influences your life, your future, how your dreams come true, the power of your imagination, how the mind works, etc.
your life will never remain the same.

www.ingramcontent.com/pod-product-compliance
Lightning Source LLC
Chambersburg PA
CBHW071123240526
45465CB00023B/794